PEARSON
PUBLISHING

Student Handbook for
Design and Technology

John Morrison

Graphics by Matthew Foster-Smith
and Emmanuel de Anda

Acknowledgement

The author is grateful to the following students for some of the coursework examples which are based on their work: Rowana Walton, Rebecca Morrison, Katie Keeble, Suzanne Edgar, James Page, Joanna Clements, Laura Pearce.

Name ....

Class...

School ....

....

Dates of exams:

1 ....

2 ....

3 ....

Exam board...

Syllabus number ....

Candidate number...

Centre number...

Further copies of this publication may be obtained from:

Pearson Publishing
Chesterton Mill, French's Road, Cambridge CB4 3NP
Tel 01223 350555   Fax 01223 356484

Email info@pearson.co.uk   Web site http://www.pearson.co.uk/education/

ISBN: 1 85749 592 6

Published by Pearson Publishing 2000
© Pearson Publishing 2000

Contents

Introduction

The aim of this handbook is to guide you through the processes involved in designing and making in a way that will build your confidence and extend your skills.

It is not intended to provide you with a set 'formula' for undertaking a design and technology project which you have to follow. Rather, it encourages an organised approach to coursework and includes a range of examples and suggestions to which you can refer to ensure you are heading in the right direction. You should still feel free to try out new ideas and challenge the conventional.

The approach to designing and making illustrated in this handbook will help KS3 students attain a high National Curriculum level.

If you are studying a GCSE course in design and technology, then the coursework design and make project will account for 60% of your final grade. This handbook will help you to improve your performance when tackling design and technology projects.

The other 40% of your marks will come from a written theory examination that tests your knowledge and understanding of the materials and processes specific to your chosen area, ie electronic products, food technology, graphic products, resistant materials technology, textiles technology, or systems and control technology. The detailed knowledge required to answer the theory exam is not contained within this handbook.

How to use this handbook

This book will help you to organise your coursework by dividing the project into a set of nine interim tasks. These tasks guide you through the stages of designing, making and evaluating and link together to enable you to complete your design folder and product.

This approach promotes good time management as it splits the project into a series of interim deadlines. The setting of interim deadlines within extended projects has been shown to cause significant improvement in student achievement.

Your teachers can customise the deadlines to meet the needs of your school.

Each interim task is set out in the following way:

1 Explaining the task and setting deadlines for completion

Each section begins by briefly explaining the task. You should also set a deadline for completion of the task. It is essential you keep to these interim deadlines. If you get behind schedule, you run the risk of not completing the coursework, or rushing later tasks and not producing your best work.

2 Help and guidance to complete the task

Additional information is then provided which will guide you through the task, explaining the key requirements and suggesting how you can include these in your work.

3 Coursework examples

Examples of project work completed by students are provided to give you a clear indication of the content and presentation of typical design sheets. These are not for you to copy but they will help in giving you examples of the approaches other students have used in their design folios. Note that these are simply *examples*; they do not claim to be 'perfect' design sheets, nor do they always exemplify every point or suggestion raised in the guidance.

4 Evaluation points

Suggestions for action and questions are included to prompt you to evaluate your work throughout the whole design and make process. Further information on evaluation is provided on page xiv.

5 Summary of task

This summarises the work you should submit to your teacher.

6 Teacher review

This provides space for your teacher to comment on your work. When you have read these comments, you should list action that you will take to improve your work further.

How you will be assessed

If you are working on your final GCSE design and make project, then this will usually count for up to 60% of your final grade. The other 40% can be gained from your written theory paper which tests your knowledge and understanding of materials and processes. Consequently, a good coursework project can set you on the road to success in this subject.

Each examination board produces their own syllabus. There is a different syllabus for each subject area of design and technology. The agreed syllabus titles for design and technology are:

- Design and Technology: Electronic Products

- Design and Technology: Food Technology

- Design and Technology: Graphic Products

- Design and Technology: Resistant Materials Technology

- Design and Technology: Textiles Technology

- Design and Technology: Systems and Control Technology.

Syllabuses are written for your teachers to help them plan their work. However, they can be useful for students as they contain examples of assessment statements that you can use to give yourself an idea of how your work is progressing. Listed on pages viii and ix are examples of assessment statements from the Assessment and Qualifications Alliance (AQA) syllabus for Design and Technology GCSE examinations. These assessment statements describe what the content of a project for grades F, D, C and A should contain. As your work progresses, read through these statements. What sort of grade do you think you are working towards? What do you need to do to improve your mark?

Assessment criteria

Candidates will have:

	Designing	Making
Grade **F**	1 used more than one source to gather research information 2 made a limited attempt to analyse the research material 3 produced a generalised specification 4 produced at least two proposals which satisfy parts of the specification 5 used a proposal, with little development, to produce the outcome 6 superficially evaluated their work against original intentions 7 demonstrated limited graphical communication and ICT skills 8 provided limited evidence of having considered industrial practices and systems and control.	1 demonstrated negligible forward planning 2 used equipment correctly and safely 3 produced a largely complete but undemanding outcome 4 demonstrated accuracy and finish in some parts of the product.
Grade **D**	1 used several appropriate sources to gather relevant research information 2 made a simple analysis of all research material 3 produced a specification which reflects most of the analysis 4 produced several proposals which satisfy the specification 5 used their proposals and relevant knowledge to develop a solution which satisfies the specification 6 evaluated, tested and modified most aspects of their work 7 used appropriate graphical communication and ICT skills to convey design ideas 8 provided limited evidence of having considered relevant industrial practices and systems and control.	1 planned sequence of making activities 2 appropriately corrected working errors 3 used appropriate equipment and processes correctly and safely 4 produced a largely complete and effective outcome 5 demonstrated a reasonable level of accuracy and finish in the product.

Designing

Making

Grade C

Designing

1. used a variety of appropriate sources to gather and order relevant research information
2. analysed the task and the research material
3. produced a specification which reflects the analysis
4. produced a range of proposals which satisfy the specification
5. used their proposals and relevant knowledge to develop a detailed design solution which satisfies the specification
6. tested, evaluated and modified their work throughout the process as appropriate
7. used a range of graphical communication and ICT skills sufficient to convey ideas to themselves and others
8. provided evidence of having considered relevant industrial practices and systems and control.

Making

1. planned the correct sequence of making activities
2. recognised the need for and justified any changes or adaptations
3. used appropriate equipment and processes correctly and safely
4. produced a complete, effective and well-assembled outcome
5. demonstrated a level of accuracy and finish in the product which satisfies most of the demands of the design solution.

Grade A

Designing

1. used a wide variety of appropriate sources to gather relevant research information
2. analysed the task and the research material logically and effectively
3. produced a detailed specification which focuses closely on the analysis
4. produced a wide range of distinct proposals which satisfy the specification
5. used one or more of their proposals and relevant knowledge of techniques, manufacturing and working characteristics to develop a detailed and coherent design solution
6. tested, objectively evaluated and effectively modified their work throughout the process as appropriate
7. selected and skillfully used a wide range of graphical communication and ICT skills which have helped to clarify their thinking and are sufficient to convey ideas to themselves and others effectively and precisely
8. provided evidence that they have considered and taken account of relevant industrial practices and systems and control.

Making

1. produced a correct sequence of activities which shows where, why and how practical production decisions were made
2. recorded and justified the need for any changes or adaptations
3. used appropriate equipment and processes consistently correctly, skilfully and safely
4. made a complete product of high quality
5. demonstrated an ability to satisfy accurately and completely all the demands of the design solution.

If you want to obtain a copy of the syllabus for your subject, you can buy one directly from the examination board. They will usually send you an order form that you complete and return with your payment. Either contact them by telephone or post, or access them via their Web site from where you can either download the syllabus or print off an order form. Your teacher will be able to tell you which syllabus your school is using. Details of the main examination boards are below:

Assessment and Qualifications Alliance (AQA, formerly AEB and NEAB)
Publications, Aldon House, 39 Heald Grove,
Rusholme, Manchester M14 4NA
or Stag Hill House, Guildford, Surrey GU2 7XJ
Tel 0161 953 1180   Fax 0161 273 7572
www.aqa.org.uk

OCR
Publications Office, Mill Wharf, Mill Street, Birmingham B6 4BU
Tel 01223 552552 Fax 01223 552553
www.ocr.org.uk

Edexcel
Edexcel Publications, Adamsway, Mansfield, Notts NG18 4FN
Tel 01623 467467   Fax 01623 450481
www.edexcel.org.uk

Welsh Joint Education Committee
245 Western Avenue, Cardiff CF5 2YX
Tel 029 2026 5000 Fax 029 2057 5994
www.wjec.co.uk

Northern Ireland Council for the Curriculum, Examinations and Assessment (CCEA)
Clarendon Dock, 29 Clarendon Road, Belfast BT1 3BG
Tel 028 9026 1205 Fax 028 9026 1233
www.ccea.org.uk

If you know how marks will be awarded for your project, then you can use this as a rough guide to channel your energies. If, for example, there are 5 marks awarded for the design brief and 45 marks awarded for initial design ideas, then you can clearly see the proportion of time and energy that needs to be applied to your design ideas. However, this is not to say that the writing of a good design brief is unimportant – quite the opposite. A well-considered design brief will set you off on the right track and help focus your design thinking.

Each of the examination boards awards different proportions of marks for your designing and making. For example, OCR awards marks to candidates under the following headings:

Objective		
1	Identification of a need leading to a design brief	*4 marks*
2	Research into design brief resulting in a specification	*12 marks*
3	Research into design brief resulting in the generation of ideas	*12 marks*
4	Product development	*12 marks*
5	Product planning and realisation	*52 marks*
6	Evaluation and testing	*8 marks*
	Spelling, punctuation and grammar	*5 marks*
		Total 105 marks

Whatever the examination board, each examination has similar stages of designing and making.

However, each of the examination boards has a different way of awarding marks for projects. **It is important that you have details of how your examination board awards the marks and that you work within their guidance.**

Managing your time

Your ability to organise your time to meet the demands of the different parts of the project is an essential part of completing your work on time and to a high standard.

Many design and technology projects are spread over a long period of time – it will help your organisation if you separate out your project into more manageable chunks of work and time.

This handbook is set out to help you focus upon these interim tasks and deadlines as a way of building up your design folder bit by bit over the timescale of your project.

Listed below are the stages of your project. Use the table on the next page to write in the dates when you have to submit your work for review by your teacher, and any targets for improvement.

Throughout this handbook, you will see boxes where you or your teacher can fill in the deadlines for each task.

The interim tasks and deadlines for your design and technology project are:

Task 1: Making a start – What should I design and make?

Task 2: The design brief

Task 3: Collecting and analysing research material to help your designing

Task 4: Producing a design specification to guide your ideas

Task 5: Design ideas – Your first thoughts

Task 6: Developing your design ideas and adding more detail

Task 7: Planning and preparing for making

Task 8: Making your chosen product

Task 9: Testing and evaluating your work.

This handbook is presented task by task with examples of students' work at each stage.

Task	Date	Targets for improvement
1		
2		
3		
4		
5		
6		
7		
8		
9		

What is evaluation?

Many students find evaluation difficult. This is often because they do not fully understand the purpose of evaluation, or because they leave it right until the end of the project. The word 'evaluation' means to make a judgement or assess the value of something.

Evaluation is a decision process you are engaged in all the time – when you make choices about which jeans to buy, which TV programme to watch or which fast-food chain to visit for a burger. You are making a decision based upon a variety of factors or criteria which may include value for money, quality of the product, entertainment value, visual appeal and, in the case of a food product, taste.

When you are designing and making, the purpose of evaluation is to try continually to improve your work. Consequently, you need to evaluate all the time – from when you select your project starting point until you finally test your finished product. You should be constantly thinking of ways to make your work more successful.

You will be involved in two different kinds of evaluation:

1   Evaluating throughout the process of designing and making. This includes evaluating the appropriateness of your starting point, your initial research, design ideas, development, plan of making and the actual making of your product.

2   You will also test and evaluate the performance of your final product. For this to be thorough, your project needs to be completed and capable of being tested and evaluated by the client, in the environment for which it was designed.

When you are working on a design and make project, your teacher or the examiner will want to see evidence of evaluation to award you the marks you deserve. One of the problems with evaluation is that you often go through the process in your mind without recording these thoughts for your teacher or the examiner. Hence, you may miss out on important marks.

To help you with this process you will find prompts throughout this handbook which are headed 'Evaluation point'. You should write down your answers to these prompts in order to create evidence of your evaluation throughout your design folder. Follow the suggestions for the type of evidence that is appropriate for each particular part of your project. Evidence of evaluation may include:

- analysis of questionnaires
- comments from the client
- photographs of the product being made
- records of testing (eg user comments or photographs).

Your own comments should also be included at each stage of the process. This evidence will help you to gain marks for each part of your work.

Task 1

Making a start – What should I design and make?

Choosing your project

In the early stages of your project you will have to establish **what** you are going to design, and for **whom** you are going to design.

Your teacher or the examination board may set your project. This may be relatively specific, eg "Design a mechanical toy for children between the ages of three and five", or it may simply be a theme, eg storage. In some ways, being set a project is easier for you, provided you are happy with the project or theme that has been set.

If you can choose your own project, then you must be careful not to spend too much time making your mind up. Use the idea generation grid on page 5. This may help you to make connections that in turn may help to jog your imagination about potential projects.

You may need to do some initial research to help you narrow down your ideas into one or a few possible starting points. You should look into the feasibility of a potential project. For example, by doing some research, you may discover that a particular project would be too complex and time-consuming to complete. (See Task 3 for more information on research.)

The next question you will need to ask yourself is which particular design and technology project will maintain your interest and enthusiasm. This will become especially important when your first burst of enthusiasm runs out and your project becomes more demanding!

If you are going to choose your own starting point, you need to ensure that your project will meet certain requirements if it is going to be successful. Check your idea against the ten points on the following pages before you proceed.

1 Does your project allow you to meet all of the assessment elements which will be used to mark your work? It will be to your disadvantage if your completed project only allows you to gain a proportion of the marks. Check with your teacher.

2 Your starting point should begin with a real design need which gives you the opportunity for lots of genuine research around the topic.

3 You should be able to produce lots of different ideas in the early stages of your designing.

4 Your project should be realistic but ambitious. It should stretch your skills in designing and making without being impossible to complete in the time available.

5 Remember that if your project is part of your GCSE coursework, you will have the pressures of other work and deadlines. If you are working in Year 9, you need to think about your SATs and other teacher assessment which will take place at the end of the year. Some students put massive amounts of time and energy into their project at the expense of their other subjects. Are you able to strike a balance?

6 How much will your project cost? It is not necessarily the case that the bigger and more expensive the project, the more marks it will receive. A small project can be an ideal opportunity to demonstrate lots of designing and making skills and it avoids all the storage, handling and expense problems associated with a larger piece of work. Are you happy that the size and cost of your project is appropriate?

7 If you design your project for someone else, eg local playgroup, hospital, elderly neighbour or company you visited on work experience, they may contribute towards the cost of materials as well as give you their opinion of your work as it progresses. Have you explored the possibility of designing for someone else?

8 Having a client is an excellent way to help you meet many of the assessment elements of your work. A client will be able to discuss your design ideas and developments as well as test and evaluate your completed product at the end of your project. Can you explain your reasons for working with or working without a client?

9 If you are following an examination course or preparing for SATs, your project will have to be completed towards the end of the spring term. This is also the time when you should be revising for written exams in this subject and others. Do not leave your work until the last minute as it will get in the way of your revision schedule. Ensure you have a suitable plan of when you will complete your work.

10 ICT should be used when it will improve your work. Examiners will be looking for examples of ways in which you have used ICT in an *appropriate* way as part of your project. Look for opportunities where ICT can help to improve your designing or making. Some of these opportunities are listed overleaf.

ICT in designing

- Research – CD-ROMs; Internet searches; TV programmes; using software to create questionnaires and analyse the responses in the form of graphs.
- Design ideas – Computer aided design (CAD) packages; graphics packages; electronic circuit design software; menu planning using a word processor or DTP package; nutrition analysis in a spreadsheet.
- Design development – Project management software; printed circuit board (PCB) design packages; modelling software.

ICT in making

Computer aided manufacture (CAM), eg:

- a plotter to produce final design plans
- a computer-controlled cutter to produce stencils for sign-writing and vinyl cutting
- iron-on stencils using standard inkjet printers
- stencils for creating glazing effect and designs
- engraving of metals, plastics and wood
- computer-controlled milling, turning and embroidery
- sewing and knitting machines.

Possible starting points

The grid opposite is designed to help you identify possible starting points for your design and technology project. Begin by selecting a possible client for your project. Then scan down the grid and link up with possible design themes. Tick any combination you would like to consider further.

Design theme \ Client	Relative	Neighbour	Local playgroup	Primary school	Local hospital	Local company	Your own school	Friend
Storage								
Educational								
Hobbies								
Furniture								
Security								
Special diets								
Display								
Graphics								
Home								
Garden								
Sport								
Fashion								
ICT								
Outdoor leisure								
Books								
Tools								

Coursework examples

Rowana explains how she decided upon her Art Deco jewellery project:

> I intend to design and make two pieces of jewellery for my elder sister Rebecca who is 22 years old. Rebecca is going to a wedding in the summer and would like me to design and make a pair of earrings and a matching brooch.

Rebecca gives the reasons for her Snack Time food project:

> As a keen sportswoman myself, I understand the need for good nutritional foods to be served in our local leisure centres.

> All sportsmen burn up calories at substantial rates, and these important calories need to be replaced. Without good nutrition, accidents and injuries can often occur. The diets that we follow, and the food that we consume, can determine how good you are at a particular sport.

> A common sight in leisure centres is a selection of vending machines, that are often full of crisps, chocolate and fizzy drinks, which only provide 'empty calories'.

> I would like to design a selection of snacks to be served in a typical leisure centre.

An example of initial thoughts and research for a rag doll on the theme 'Life at sea' is given on page 7.

Rag Doll

Life at Sea
Initial Thoughts

Sailor

Cliffs

Seaside

Buoy

Life at sea

Sea life
– fish
– sea shells
– seaweed

Lighthouse

Seagulls

Boats

Rag doll ideas

- Starfish
- Sailor
- Boat
- Dolphin
- Tropical fish

Task 1 Action

Evaluation point

Make notes on your reasons for choosing your project.
Why do think your product is necessary?

For whom are you designing, and why?

Summary of what you need to submit

If you are choosing your own topic, or are choosing a project
based around a given theme, write out a brief proposal for your
teacher to review.

Teacher review

Date submitted:

Teacher comments:

Targets for improvement:

Task 2

The design brief

What is a design brief?

Your design brief is simply a clear statement of your intent. It is a written piece in which you explain a number of issues surrounding your project. It should include and expand upon the points you made in your initial proposal (see Task 1) and should clearly explain what you are going to design.

As mentioned on page 1, you might arrive at your project idea in a number of different ways. Here are a few examples:

- Your teacher may set you a design for which you have to produce your own ideas. For example, you are required to design and make a decorative frame that will display a number of photographs.

- You may be given a starting point or theme that you have to interpret to meet your own needs. Examples of such themes might include storage, body adornment or healthy eating.

- You may identify a need from which you create your own design brief. For example, you have a grandparent who loves gardening but finds it difficult to carry heavy loads. Can you design and make a product that might ease the problem?

Listed below are examples of some of the issues you might include in your design brief. You could write a sentence or two about any that are appropriate to your project. You may also add extra points.

- Who is the client(s)/user(s) for whom you are intending to design? (A photograph of the client and/or situation will bring the project to life.)

- Explain why you chose this particular design project. If the brief was given by your teacher, explain how you intend to interpret it.

- Explain the problem that you are investigating. For example, your grandmother likes gardening but finds it difficult to carry her tools. What are you designing to help her? How will your product provide a suitable solution?

- Explain where and when your completed project might be used.

- How will you meet the needs of your client(s) with your chosen project?

- What type of research will you need to help develop your design ideas? (See Task 3 for information on research.)

- How will you present your designs to the client(s)/user(s)? How will you gather and record their opinions?

- When your project is finished, how will you test and evaluate your work?

Coursework examples

An example of a design brief for jewellery based around ideas from different design periods is given on page 11.

A design brief based on the theme of storage is provided on page 12.

Page 13 shows a design brief for a project set by the teacher.

DESIGN BRIEF

I intend to design and make two pieces of jewellery for my elder sister Rebecca who is 22 years old. Rebecca is going to a wedding in the summer and would like me to design and make a pair of earrings, a necklace and a matching brooch which will be based around a theme we will agree following my research.

I will decide on my approach when she has decided what she is going to wear, and once I have completed my initial research of design periods such as Art Nouveau, Art Deco and the Bauhaus. As I will be making my jewellery in metal, I will also need to research the properties of different metals and methods of construction and finish, as well as collecting and analysing examples of different jewellery from books, magazines and the Internet.

When the jewellery is finished, I will ask my sister to try it on with her wedding outfit. I will photograph her wearing the jewellery and write down her opinion of the completed objects. I will also ask other members of my family as to their views about my work.

Design Brief

The problem

My bedroom is often left untidy with my CDs lying around the floor and furniture. I am often being nagged by my mother to tidy up. I need somewhere to keep these items.

What am I going to do about this?

The brief

I am going to design and make a storage unit to hold thirty CDs. I want this unit to be transportable so that I can take it with me when visiting friends. It must have some way of keeping dust out in order to keep my CDs clean. It would also be useful to have some sort of lock on the unit to prevent my little brother from borrowing these items. I want this unit to blend in with the existing furniture in the room.

Design Brief

Design a toy for children between the ages of three and five years old. Remember to consider the materials available to you and the costs. The toy must be mechanical in some way.

To complete and answer this design brief I am going to have to design a toy to match the limitations above. To complete the brief successfully I am going to research into many different areas: available and suitable materials; analysis of toys that are presently on the market; various mechanisms to find the mechanisms which would be best suited for my toy.

I have also decided for extra research to write to some of the leading toy companies on the market:

Fisher Price Ltd, PO Box 100, Peterlee SR1 2RF

Early Learning Centre, South Marston Park, Swindon SN3 4TJ

London Toy Company, Unit 180, Alexandra Avenue, Harrow HA2 9BN

Once I have drawn my initial ideas, I will choose my final idea and select the best materials to use. I will then make and complete my final design. I will test the toy on both adults and children, as it would be parents who would have to buy the toy.

Task 2 Action

Evaluation point

Make notes on your client's opinion of your design brief. Do you
need to change it in any way?

Summary of what you need to submit

1   A written design brief which accurately explains your project.

2   A plan of research (see pages 16 and 17) which is based on your
    initial analysis of the design brief and guides you towards collecting
    information about your topic.

Teacher review

Date submitted:

Teacher comments:

Targets for improvement:

Task 3

Collecting and analysing
research material

What is research?

Research is concerned with finding out what you need to know to
help you design and make your project. It will often involve you
finding information about topics and issues that may be new to
you. Do not be put off by, or worried about, exploring these new
areas of knowledge. When taking on the role of a designer you
need to get used to the idea of being continually challenged by
uncertainties. As you collect your research, you should begin to see
ways in which you can make imaginative connections which will
help to shape your initial design ideas.

Research, and your analysis of your research, is an important part of
your project, as it should help to focus your design thinking. How
many times have you looked at a successful product and wondered
"That's a good design… I wonder where the idea came from?" In
many cases, the answer to this may have been based around the
designer's curiosity and the ideas that were created as a result of
their research around the topic.

Firstly, you have to decide on the type of research that will help
you with your project. You may find it useful to produce a plan of
research that will include a list of what you need to know and
where you might collect that information. Always discuss your
proposals with your teacher, friends and parents to see if you have
missed any obvious areas of research. However, you can always do
extra research as your project progresses if you need to find out
additional information.

An example of part of a plan of research for a jewellery design is given below:

What research I need to collect	Type of research	Where I might find the information
Illustrations of Egyptian styles	Pictures	Library books, CD-ROMs, museum Web sites
Working properties of copper, brass, nickel and silver	Written notes and test pieces	D&T textbooks and workshop experiments
Preferences of my clients	Interview or questionnaire	Discussion with clients
Costs of materials	Notes	Ask teacher, ring metal suppliers, check Web sites

An example of a research plan for a rag doll based on a choice of themes is provided on pages 24 and 25.

Examples of different types of research are as follows:

- Picture research
- Collecting people's opinions
- Visits
- Writing letters to ask for information
- Reading, including using the Internet
- Product analysis, or analysis of particular components or processes.

Picture research

This might include examples of similar products to those you are intending to design. It may also include illustrations of buildings, patterns or natural objects, such as plants, or any other pictures that will help you to think about your design. You can photocopy or scan images from books and magazines or access Web sites and CD-ROMs relating to your topic.

Make a note of where you take any pictures from so that you can credit the sources.

You can use pictures to help you sketch shapes and styles which might fit in with your planned design. You can take patterns and styles that you can use as starting points for your design sheets. However, always be careful that you are not copying someone else's work.

An example of picture research is given on pages 26 and 27.

Collecting people's opinions

If you want to collect opinions from a lot of people, then it is worthwhile devising a questionnaire that you can hand out to them. You might include this as part of your research if you wanted to identify, for example, people's favourite food, most popular type of wood, preferred colour of fabric, or the maximum costs someone might pay for your product.

If you only want to collect the views of one person, you can arrange an interview with the person concerned and record their views. This might be a good technique to use with your client when you are trying to clarify exactly what they need.

Designing and writing a questionnaire

Writing a questionnaire offers a good opportunity for you to use some information and communication technology in your project. Software is available which can be used to design, collate and analyse information. This software has three distinct parts:

- The first allows you to design the questionnaire which will be given out to those you hope will answer your questions – ie the respondents.

- The second allows you to fill in the answers you have received to enable you to build a database of responses.

- The third uses the computer to analyse the data you have collected and present it in graphical form, including bar charts, pie charts, scatter graphs, etc.

How to design your questionnaire

Designing your questionnaire will be easier if you have a clear idea of the type of information you want to collect to help inform your design thinking as the project develops.

- Put a clear title at the top of the questionnaire.

- Give clear instructions to the respondents to help them answer your questionnaire correctly. Do they have to tick a box, underline an answer, select a date or write a sentence? You will waste a lot of time if your respondents answer the questionnaire incorrectly because they do not understand how to complete the answers.

- Your first questions could gather some information about the respondent answering your questionnaire. This might include details about their age group and sex.

For example:

> **1 What age group are you in?**
> Place a tick in the box opposite your age group:
>
> ☐ 6 to 10 years   ☐ 11 to 13 years
> ☐ 14 to 16 years   ☐ 17 to 19 years
> ☐ 20 to 25 years   ☐ Over 25 years

Note that by asking the respondents to identify an age group, rather than writing their specific age, it will be easier to analyse the answers in blocks for graphic display.

You can now begin to write specific questions relating to your project. It is a good idea to write out your questions in draft form first and try them out with a friend or teacher to ensure your questions are easily understood and do not have more than one meaning. List below some possible questions you may wish to include in your questionnaire:

1 ....

....

2 ....

....

3 ....

....

4 ....

....

An example questionnaire, and its analysis, is provided on pages 28 and 29.

Visits

Visits you might make could include the following:

- **Client** – To discuss the initial idea and obtain their views as the project develops.

- **Specialist shops** – Useful for product analysis, ie comparing and contrasting similar products to your project. For example, supermarkets may be useful for food products; Mothercare can help with toy design and children's clothes; DIY stores can help with information about security devices; IKEA has lots of examples of product design, furniture and textiles.

- **Shops** – Useful for finding out about types of materials, their availability, their cost and how they are used.

- **Museums** – For finding out about the historical background to your product, if appropriate.

- **Libraries** – To look at books about your topic. Make notes or photocopy pictures and information to use as part of your research or for developing ideas.

- **Work experience** – You may be able to use a work experience contact as a client. Most companies need brochures, company logos and professionally-designed headed notepaper for letters, orders and invoices. Hence, this might offer opportunities for graphic design.

- **Nurseries, playgroups and schools** – Good, when designing educational toys, for gaining 'expert' advice and data from the children, as well as from their teacher/supervisor.

Writing letters

You could write a letter to a company to request:

- information about their products
- a visit to observe how they manufacture products
- an interview with a designer.

Writing a letter to an organisation or company can be effective if you have a named individual to write to, or you know that the company has a specialist education officer. However, do not get frustrated if your letters are not answered.

Reading

By reading books, newspapers, magazines, brochures etc, and accessing CD-ROMS and the Internet, you can gain a lot of information to help you improve your understanding of particular topics, and some useful resources.

Remember just to extract the particular illustrations or information that are useful for your project. Be selective. When you come to write up your research, do not include information just to pad out your project. Use only *appropriate* pictures, text and information and write brief notes alongside your research explaining how this has helped your thinking.

An example of this kind of research is given on pages 30 and 31.

Examples of useful Web sites are listed on page 107.

Product analysis

When you are designing a new product about which you know very little, it is a good idea to analyse similar products to improve your level of understanding. You could begin by sketching or photographing a similar product and getting to know its main characteristics. Look at the way it is made and the materials, components or ingredients involved in its construction.

You could organise a consumer test where you try out the product and make judgements about its advantages and disadvantages. Ask others to try it out and give their opinion.

You could also make judgements about the visual appeal of the product or its overall performance, perhaps based around evidence you have collected via a questionnaire.

Product analysis builds up your own knowledge and understanding and prepares you to tackle the design issues surrounding your project.

Examples of product and component analysis are provided on pages 32 to 35.

How to analyse and use your research

When you analyse the research material you have collected, you need to look in detail and with care at each piece of information or picture to select what is relevant to your project. This process of analysis will help you to discover more meaning about the topic you are studying and will inform your design thinking.

For example, you might visit the British Standards Institution (BSI) Web site to collect information about the safety issues surrounding children's pull-along toys. The BSI issues specific requirements that need to be met by any toy produced. A pull-along cord, for example, "must be more than 1.5 mm thick" and should "not have any knots or fastenings which could make a slip-knot".

These two pieces of information will be of benefit to a design specification for a pull-along toy as they can go directly into the list of requirements. The information will directly influence your designing as you know what the minimum diameter of the cord must be and that it must not have any knots or fastenings as part of its construction.

An example of analysis of research undertaken is provided on pages 36 and 37.

Presenting your research and analysis

Once you have completed your research, you will need to begin to organise your pictures and text ready to mount up into your design folder. As your sheets illustrating your research gradually emerge, you need to make notes explaining how this material has informed your choices and enabled you to make judgements.

Remember that you can still collect and use additional research as your work progresses. This might help you in the later stages of your project when you are finding out more details about material costs, methods of construction and from where items can be bought.

Rag Doll

Research Plan

I need to find as much visual information about the themes listed in the brief. Then I need to identify one theme and gather specific information about that theme. I need to look at individual items of clothing, including accessories. I also need to work out how they are made.

Craft shops

CD-ROM encyclopedia

Places to look for ideas

Library

School textbooks

Clothing, shoes, etc to see how they are made

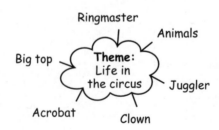

Ringmaster

Animals

Big top

Theme: Life in the circus

Juggler

Acrobat

Clown

Farm animals:
Chicks
Sheep
Pigs
Cows, etc

Checked shirt

Wellies

Dress

Theme:
Life in the
country

Straw hat

Dungarees

Countryside:
windmills
animals
rocks
rivers
bridges

Research

The first thing you notice about 'Sly the Fox' is the wild use of colour. The picture practically leaps off the page. Colours make the picture exciting for the reader. I think the fox is a little unrealistic because it's blue. I would have made it orange. The expression is funny for children. Sly the Fox is drawn simplistically.

The books about 'Max the Cat' were always favourites of mine as a child. Even now, the pictures draw you in. The cat's big smile, the huge whiskers and the big paws all add a nice little touch. Children like little details and I think the attention to detail on the cat's fur is good.

Emmanuel de Anda's pictures have a special quality that children and adults adore. He has an effortless style. The pictures jump off the page at you. They are very simple but still look good. The drawings are imaginative and never lack interest. Maybe children love Emmanuel's pictures because they are almost as if a child has drawn them. They are very funny and everyone loves his unique style.

Snack Time!

Leisure Centre Questionnaire

1 How many hours of exercise do you do each week?
☐ 1 ☐ 2 ☐ 3 ☐ 4 ☐ 5 ☐ 6

2 What kind of sport do you participate in most often?
☐ Football ☐ Netball ☐ Swimming
☐ Rugby ☐ Tennis ☐ Weight training
☐ Other ....

3 What food do you snack on most after exercise?
☐ Chocolate ☐ Crisps ☐ Salad
☐ Fizzy pop ☐ Sandwich ☐ Pie/sausage roll

4 Why do you snack on these foods?
☐ They taste good ☐ They're cheap
☐ They fill you up ☐ They're easy to eat

5 How often do you visit a local leisure centre?
☐ Never ☐ Sometimes
☐ Once a week ☐ Twice a week or more

6 If you were to eat at a leisure centre, which of the following would you like to see on the menu? (please select three only)
☐ pizza/quiche ☐ salad
☐ pasta dish ☐ fresh sandwiches
☐ jacket potatoes ☐ main meals, eg stir-fry, etc

Results

Top three answers:

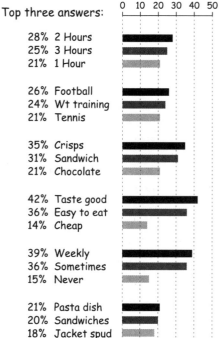

%	Answer
28%	2 Hours
25%	3 Hours
21%	1 Hour
26%	Football
24%	Wt training
21%	Tennis
35%	Crisps
31%	Sandwich
21%	Chocolate
42%	Taste good
36%	Easy to eat
14%	Cheap
39%	Weekly
36%	Sometimes
15%	Never
21%	Pasta dish
20%	Sandwiches
18%	Jacket spud

Conclusion from Research

I intend to concentrate on creating pasta dishes, sandwiches and jacket potatoes with fillings, since these were the most preferred dishes. The answers to question 4 show me that my dishes need to taste good and be easy to eat. They should also be reasonably priced.

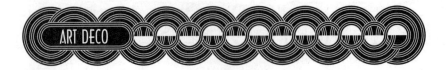

RESEARCH

The term Art Deco was created after an exhibition in Paris in 1966 called 'Les Années '25'. The exhibition concentrated on the twenties and the 1925 Paris Exposition Internationale des Arts Décoratifs et Industriels Modernes. The term Art Deco is, however, applied loosely to the period between the wars.

The greatest influence on Art Deco jewellery was pre-World War One Parisian fashion. Paul Poiret transformed female dress design. He freed the female figure from the restraints of the Victorian corset and designed dresses that were long, tubular and without much adornment. This look needed a similarly simple, minimal line of jewellery.

To accentuate the vertical line of the long dresses, jewellery designers introduced long, dangling necklaces. Strings of pearls and beads were worn down the back, over one shoulder or wrapped around one arm. Necklaces suspended with pendants and tassels hung as far as the stomach or sometimes even to the knees.

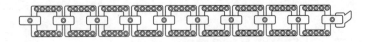

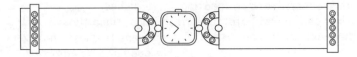

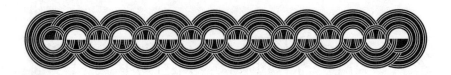

Because in the First World War all the heavy fabrics were needed for the troops, women had to use lighter materials like rayon and muslin. This had an impact on the design of jewellery, calling for lighter designs which were often mounted in platinum.

As the style of dress was sleeveless, several new designs of bracelets evolved. The most popular were flat, flexible narrow bands decorated with compact, stylised designs of flowers, geometric patterns or exotic motifs. The watch bracelet was also popularised.

By day, the wristwatch was plain with a leather or ribbon strap and by night it resembled a richly jewelled bracelet set with pearls and diamonds mounted in either enamelled or bi-coloured gold.

The principal motifs in Art Deco jewellery design were simple geometric shapes — the square, circle, triangle, etc. These were often overlapped or placed next to each other to create complex configurations.

Snack Time!

The Facts on Veggie

Below are two tables. One contains the nutritional value for Bolognese sauce with Veggie sausages, and the other for Bolognese with minced beef.

Minced Beef Bolognese

Ingredients	Energy (kJ)	Energy (kcal)	Protein (g)	Fat (g)
500g minced beef	1990	458	46.2	30.4
1 onion	40	10	0.6	
3 carrots	160	40	1.2	
Can tomatoes	200	48	4.0	
100g mushrooms	60	15	2.0	0.6
Total	2450	571	54.0	31.0

Veggie Bolognese

Ingredients	Energy (kJ)	Energy (kcal)	Protein (g)	Fat (g)
500g Veggie	710	170	24.6	6.4
1 onion	40	10	0.6	
3 carrots	160	40	1.2	
Can tomatoes	200	48	4.0	
100g mushrooms	60	15	2.0	0.6
Total	1170	283	32.4	7.0

The makers of Veggie have told us that Veggie is extremely healthy, but just how healthy is Veggie really?

the food of the future

Veggie™

SAUSAGES

LOW in FAT

6 succulent meat-free sausages with a unique herby flavour

As you can see from my results, there is quite a difference between Veggie and real meat.

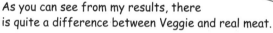

There is nearly five times as much fat in the beef bolognese compared to the Veggie bolognese. This could make many customers buy Veggie instead of beef mince especially if the buyer is on a diet.

Also in the beef bolognese, there are 571 kcal. If you compare this to the Veggie bolognese, you can see that there are half as many kcal in the Veggie bolognese. Once again, the Veggie is better if you are 'counting your calories'.

The tables helped me with my studies on Veggie. The main reason why people choose Veggie instead of meat is because they are vegetarian and need other sources of protein. Veggie's major downfall is that it contains half as much protein compared to meat.
Veggie may be the 'food of the future' but it still doesn't contain as much protein as meat.

Veggie™

the food of the future

Research

Here are some of the mechanisms and materials I looked closely at.

Mechanisms

Rack and pinion
Rotating to linear

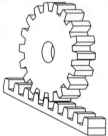

Peg and slot
Rotating to oscillating

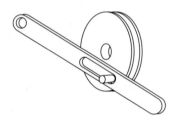

Materials

Useful properties

Mild steel
Alloy of iron and carbon

Easily worked and machined. It can be joined by brazing, welding, and the use of screw threads and rivets. It is inexpensive and available in many forms: thin rod, tube, strip and flat sheet.

Acrylic
Polymethyl Methacrylate

Stain and moisture-resistant. It is easily worked and shaped and can be formed by heat. It is attractive and available in a variety of colours.

Brass
Alloy of copper and zinc

It machines well and can be used for parts of the project which need precision. Its 'gold'-like appearance can provide a pleasant contrast if used alongside wood or acrylic.

Aluminium

Soft, lightweight, easy to work, bend and polish.

Mechanical Toy

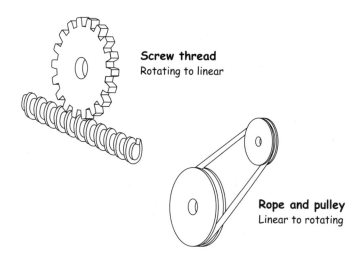

Screw thread
Rotating to linear

Rope and pulley
Linear to rotating

Disadvantages

Easily rusts and will not withstand condensation problems, unless it is either chromium-plated, plastic-coated or protected in some other way.

Acrylic can be brittle, and holes should not be drilled too close together. The edges need to be carefully polished if it is to look its best – this can be time-consuming.

Expensive, easily discolours and tarnishes if not constantly polished or protected with a 'lacquer'.

Very difficult to join by soldering or welding without specialised equipment.

Toy Electronic Keyboard

Analysis of Market Research

I analysed each category of each organ researched.

Physical Attributes

Of the physical attributes, I particularly looked at size. The keyboards were between 200 mm and 450 mm long, the larger organs having as many as four octaves and the small organs having a minimum of one octave. Bearing in mind that most of these keyboards were designed for children younger than seven years old, with smaller hands, this suggests that my organ will be between 300 mm and 400 mm long.

Most of the keyboards had only one speaker; this might suffice, but two might be necessary to appeal to the older age group.

Colourwise, the keyboards fell into three categories: those in primary colours aimed at young children below seven years; the themed organs aimed at a specific group; and the conventional black and white organs with limited appeal to children.

The last physical attribute that I highlighted was a handle; only two organs had this feature but I consider it to be a particularly useful one.

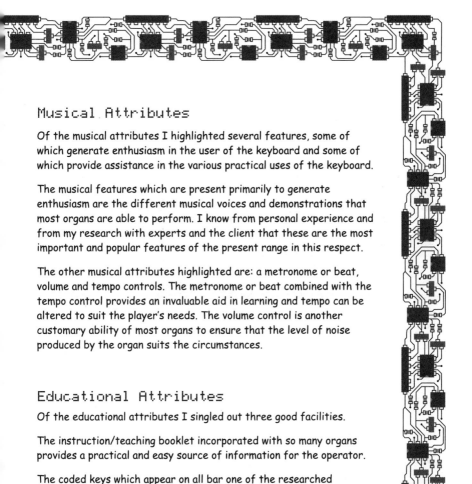

Musical Attributes

Of the musical attributes I highlighted several features, some of which generate enthusiasm in the user of the keyboard and some of which provide assistance in the various practical uses of the keyboard.

The musical features which are present primarily to generate enthusiasm are the different musical voices and demonstrations that most organs are able to perform. I know from personal experience and from my research with experts and the client that these are the most important and popular features of the present range in this respect.

The other musical attributes highlighted are: a metronome or beat, volume and tempo controls. The metronome or beat combined with the tempo control provides an invaluable aid in learning and tempo can be altered to suit the player's needs. The volume control is another customary ability of most organs to ensure that the level of noise produced by the organ suits the circumstances.

Educational Attributes

Of the educational attributes I singled out three good facilities.

The instruction/teaching booklet incorporated with so many organs provides a practical and easy source of information for the operator.

The coded keys which appear on all bar one of the researched products also provide a source of useful knowledge. As a musician, I favour the letter, stave and scale coded keys.

The last feature, that I know from research and experience provides a useful method of practice, is the recording and playback facility.

Task 3 Action

Evaluation point

Discuss the outcomes of your research and comment upon those areas which have been most useful and explain why. Which parts of your research have been less useful? Explain why.

Evaluate your research. What has been really useful in helping your design thinking and what has not been so productive? Has your research helped to resolve any problems or concerns?

Summary of what you need to submit

A number of research sheets that include your own comments about and analysis of the material you have collected.

Teacher review

Date submitted:

Teacher comments:

Targets for improvement:

Task 4

Producing a design
specification

What is a design specification?

A design specification is a list of requirements that your completed
design product should meet if it is to be successful. This may
involve details about the needs of the client(s)/user(s).

You could begin your specification by writing down what the
product is intended to do. You could then use your research
conclusions to form the starting point for each specification, eg
"From my measurements of people's arm lengths, I discovered that
the arm rest should be 25-40 cm long".

Try to use measurable statements, eg "Each snack should contain
10 g or more of protein" rather than "Each snack should be high
in protein".

One of the biggest challenges you will have when writing your
design specification is to identify all of the issues or requirements
you need to consider when you start to design. Successful products
have to meet a complete range of technical and visual
requirements. The skill of the professional designer is to create a
product that meets the needs of the user at a price that offers
good value for money. Your skill will be in designing and making a
product that meets the needs of your client.

Many products will have to meet similar requirements or elements.
Safety issues will nearly always apply to any product you are trying
to design. Hence, your design specification should always have a
number of points relating to safety or hygiene.

For example, in a design for children's pyjamas, two points in your design specification relating to the material to be used might be:

- the fabric should be easy to wash
- the fabric should be flame-retardant.

In writing your design specification, you are setting yourself some guidelines to help you check the effectiveness of your emerging design ideas and ensure they meet your client's needs.

It might be helpful to think about a number of **broad design elements** that *any* product might have to meet if it is to be successful. Then think about specific points that your design would have to meet within these design elements. These can guide you in producing a personalised product design specification.

Listed below and on the following pages, you will find 18 design elements which could be part of any product specification.

Note that not all elements will apply to your product. On the other hand, in some cases, a number of specifications may emerge from a single element. For example, when you consider the visual requirements of your product, you could write individual specifications about colour, shape, style, form and texture.

Using the following questions as prompts, write a personalised statement about the design elements that apply to your project. As guidance, you will find an example of a specification after most of the elements.

1 Are there any **safety** or **hygiene** issues that your product must meet?

The quality of finish on my wooden toy must comply with the British Standard for Toys which states 'The surface of wooden toys shall not be rough to such an extent that risk of injury from splinters shall result'.

2 Will you have to design any special features into your product to prepare it for the **environment** in which it will be used?

The towel rail I am designing for the bathroom will have to withstand high levels of condensation and humidity.

3 How will the product be **tested**?

When I have completed my three vegetarian meals, I will ask my auntie, who is acting as my client, to write her comments about my dishes.

4 Has the product got a limited **shelf-life**?

My cooked chilled pasta dish will need to be refrigerated below 5°C and eaten within two days of making.

5 How should the product be **stored**?

The small goalposts I am designing for the local infants' school must fold flat when not in use.

6 Does the product need to be **packaged**?

My adventure game will need to be packaged in a container to ensure all the pieces do not get mixed up and to allow the outside of the packaging to be used to promote the game to potential buyers.

7 Will you need to produce any **instructions** to help people use your product?

My booklet describing the use of the child's electronic organ will contain instructions for changing the batteries, tuning each key and examples of tunes which can be easily played.

8 What are the **properties of the materials** you will use when making your final product?

The sports top I am designing should be made from fabric that is crease-resistant, lightweight and showerproof.

9 Will your product need to have a **protective finish**?

The rack I am designing for the back of my bike will have to have a finish that protects it from corrosion in wet weather.

10 Will your product need to meet any **ergonomic** or **anthropometric** requirements?

You need to understand what these two terms mean and whether they are relevant to your project. Once you are clear about this, you can research the particular area of ergonomics and anthropometrics which will help your designing. Definitions and examples are as follows:

Ergonomics – This is the study of the way the human body interacts with designed products, architecture and environments. For example:

- What makes a chair comfortable?

- Why maintain an even temperature in offices?

- How do you ensure a desk lamp gives you adequate lighting without glare?

- How do you make the time setting display on a microwave oven easy to read?

You should begin by researching relevant ergonomic details and then discuss them with your client to find out their preferences.

Anthropometrics – This relates to detailed dimensions of the human body, for example, the variations in the length of leg in men, women and children of various ages. Further examples include:

- What is a suitable height for a classroom chair to be used by five to six year olds?

- What is the most suitable height for a dining table?

- What is the minimum size of touch key you would use on a mobile phone?

11 Are there any **British Standards** that your product will need to meet if it is to be successful?

The British Standards Institution is an organisation that produces guidelines or minimum standards which many materials and products must reach. All standards are given a number that helps you to identify them, rather like a registration number on a car, eg BS4163 relates to safety guidelines for design and technology departments in schools.

With the emergence of the single European Market, many of the British Standards have merged with European Standards. This includes the British Standard for Toys, known as BSEN71. This means the standard is both a British (BS) and European (EN) Standard.

For more details refer to the BSI Web site at: **http://www.bsi.org.uk/education/**

12 What **visual requirements** will your product have to meet?

The jewellery I am designing will be based around the theme of the Art Deco style.

13 Will your product have to meet specific **performance** requirements?

The electronic timing circuit must be capable of being set for five minutes, after which an audible and visual signal will be given to indicate that the time has passed.

14 Does your product have to meet precise **cost** limits?

The cost of the food ingredients for my vegetarian snack should not exceed £1.50 per person.

15 Does your product have to meet specific **size** requirements?

The sports shorts I am designing must have a 28-inch waist.

16 Is there a minimum or maximum **weight** that your product must meet? Is there a desirable weight? Do you need to include handles to aid lifting?

The storage case for my laptop computer should not weigh more than 150 grams. It should include a handle and a shoulder strap.

17 Are you **limited** by **specific materials** and **processes** that will restrict your facilities for making?

I will have to make my tray from acrylic as this material can be shaped and formed by the tools and processes we have in school. However, in an industrial context, it could be made from glass-reinforced plastic or injection-moulded using polypropylene.

18 If your product needs to be maintained, how can you design these features into your work?

In the construction of the case to house the electronic circuitry for my musical organ, I will need to ensure there is easy access to change the batteries.

Writing a successful design specification and agreeing this with your client is a very important part of your project as it sets up the framework within which you are going to design and make.

Some points in your specification will be more important than others. For example, if you were a car designer, it would be essential that the vehicle had an efficient braking system. Customers and safety standards would **demand** this. However, whether the car was fitted with air-conditioning or not would be the **wish** of individual customers.

In a similar way you should see your product design specification as having **demands** and **wishes**. It is essential that you design to meet all the demands, and it is desirable that you meet as many wishes as you can.

However, *do not* consider your initial design specification to be a rigid set of rules that cannot be revised. It may well be that, as your project develops, some of your elements will need to be reviewed and modified to improve the overall success of the final product. This is all part of the ongoing evaluation of your work and is a necessary element in the design process.

Coursework examples

Two examples of design specifications, for a piece of jewellery and a child's storybook, are given on pages 46 and 47.

ART DECO

SPECIFICATION

1 The item of jewellery needs to be designed in the Art Deco style.

The chosen materials do not need to be waterproof but need to be comfortable to wear. 2

3 There shouldn't be any sharp corners or rough edges.

The jewellery needs to be lightweight and durable. 4

5 The materials shouldn't cost more than £15.

The jewellery needs to be attractive and versatile. 6

7 The jewellery could be made out of a lightweight wood.

The design should be of a geometric style using simple shapes and designs. 8

9 There needs to be some kind of mechanism so that the separate items can articulate around each other.

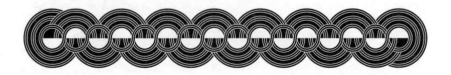

Storybook

Specification

I intend to make a mock-up children's book which will fulfil my client's needs.

○ Illustrations are very important because, as my client said, "a picture tells a thousand words," and "it gives a child clues when learning to read". Therefore, my illustrations will need to be clear and should add to the text.

○ The book will need to be colourful to attract the child's attention and make the illlustrations more interesting and vivid. I will use a variety of colours, but especially green, purple, pink, yellow and red as my research revealed these to be the most popular colours of the children questioned.

○ The pictures should be bold and simple, yet include detail. I have found from my research that children like detail. It gives them something extra to look at and draws them in.

○ I am going to use a variety of themes taken from some favourite children's books. The book should be funny and also a bit scary, with adventure, mystery and animal characters. The storyline also needs careful attention. The illustrations need to fit the themes.

○ Facial expressions will mean a lot, so I need to make sure that they're effective. They need to be realistic, but with an element of humour.

○ The pictures must not take over the text but should stand out and be noticed.

Task 4 Action

Evaluation point

As your specification develops, ask your client to evaluate it to see if it meets their needs.

What did your client like/dislike about your design specification? Have you added any additional design elements to your specification following discussion with your client?

Summary of what you need to submit

A detailed design specification that includes all the elements specific to your particular design project.

Teacher review

Date submitted:

Teacher comments:

Targets for improvement:

Task 5

Design ideas –
Your first thoughts

Initial design thoughts

When you begin putting your initial design thoughts down on paper you should concentrate on producing a whole range of ideas. The emphasis at this stage is to show a wide variety of proposals without the need to concentrate on too much detail.

The main difficulty you may have is how to trigger these ideas. Sitting down with a blank sheet of paper and expecting to pull ideas out of your own imagination is difficult for most people, and very few, if any, designers work in this way. You need material to refer to which will give you inspiration, expand your thinking and make the task of designing that much easier.

Stimulating design thinking

Whatever design topic you choose, you will find that there is a huge variety of books which focus on or around your theme. Begin by browsing through the books and perhaps photocopying relevant pages to help your design thinking. Be careful not to copy directly though – not only will this gain you fewer marks but you may be breaking copyright by doing so! If you are unsure, ask your teacher.

You need to have visual material or research information that will stimulate your thought processes. On pages 52 and 53 you will see a number of designs for jewellery which were inspired by simple geometric shapes from the Art Deco period.

It is at this stage of the project that the efforts you have put into your research will be rewarded. Good quality research will support good quality design ideas.

What should be included in my initial designs?

As you begin to set out your design ideas, try to produce as many ideas as possible. Some will develop into more advanced designs, whilst you may decide that others are not worth developing any further. However, ensure that all your ideas, both good and not so good, are recorded on your design sheets. Do not throw away marks by editing out your weaker proposals. All work at this stage is worthy of consideration and will gain you valuable marks.

Refer to your design brief, research and design specification when generating design ideas. Your ideas can include solutions to parts of the whole product – they do not all have to be a fully-functioning total product. It may also be that some parts of the product only have one sensible design solution so do not waste time producing unnecessary variety.

You can use computer-aided design packages to help present your initial ideas. However, it may be quicker, easier and more appropriate to use hand-drawn sketches and diagrams. Make sure that your ideas are clearly presented and your main points are highlighted.

Examples of initial designs are included on pages 52 to 60.

Evaluating your ideas

Record in note form alongside your design ideas any thoughts or opinions you have about your work. These notes or annotations are important ways in which you communicate your thoughts and opinions about your work to your teacher or the examiner. These annotations are evidence that you are thinking about your work and making judgements about your ideas. This process is part of your own evaluation of your work and is one of the ways in which designers strive to improve the quality of their designs. Listed below you will find examples of questions you can ask yourself about your work to help trigger your evaluations:

- Does this idea meet the requirements of your original design brief?

- Explain why you have rejected this idea or why this idea is worthy of further development.

- What evidence from your research have you used in your designing?

- What decisions have you made?

- How might your idea be improved?

- Is your idea visually appealing? How might you make it more visually appealing?

List alongside your ideas the type of materials you would intend to use during the making stages of your project. Are these materials available, or will you need to adapt your design to fit in with what is available in school?

ART DECO

INITIAL DESIGNS

All the designs on this page are
for the necklace chain links.

I started off simply with basic circles, triangles
and squares. The links would be made of metal.

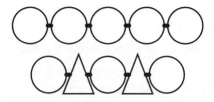

I then started to make the links thicker and explored
more shapes. I like the first idea better as the difference
between the thickness of links looks more balanced.

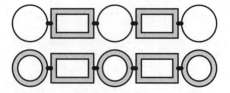

The shaded areas show where there could be different-coloured stone or metal.

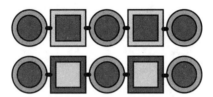

Out of the following two ideas, I prefer the second one because the colours are more symmetrical and balanced than the first.

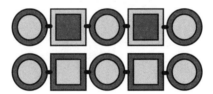

The second idea is thin metal links which will be overlapped. I don't really like it, but it would meet the client's needs.

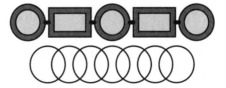

I thought this dinosaur would be a fun toy to play with. The drawing is from a side view. As the dinosaur rolls along the floor, I would like his mouth to open and close. The cam of the dinosaur would be off-centred to the right. He would be made out of wood.

This train would be pulled along the floor. The people would be linked to a cam and would pop out as it is rolled along.

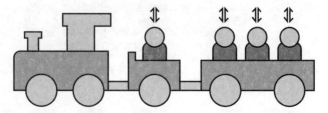

Mechanical Toy

Initial Ideas

This is a simple figure. I will adapt his feet to be round wooden cylinders, so he can roll or be pushed along the ground. As he rolls, I would like his hat to go up and down.

The duck would have wooden wheels at its base. When pushed along, his wings would go up and down.

style café

initial designs

I designed this café around the name 'The Coffee House', because I liked it so much. I wanted a café for late nights which is why I chose red, blue and white as my main colours. I used pens and paint because they are so much bolder and stronger than crayons. I am not convinced that this café fulfils the brief as I feel it is too sophisticated for teenagers and I probably would not visit it with my friends.

However, my client felt differently. She thought it was attractively rich and the sort of place with no children where you meet people. She said it looked smart and had a very subdued and intimate atmosphere. I can see her point but do not feel I would visit this café so I have decided to reject this idea.

To improve on this design and make it look more appealing to teenagers like me, I would mainly focus on changing the door and windows, and get rid of the plants, although I would keep the colours as I quite like the atmosphere they portray.

style café

initial designs

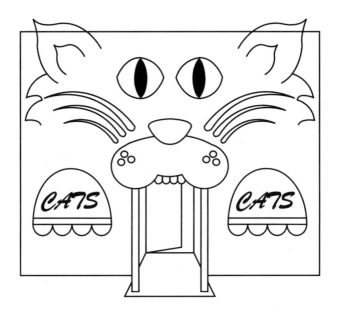

I wanted all of my designs to be totally different, each with their own theme and I believe this design has fulfilled my aim. However, although this café is visually attractive, it does not fulfil my brief. This is because my client feels it is only appealing to children and cat lovers! I agree with this however fun it is. My client does feel that it is inviting though and very unique.

To improve this café, I would make it more appealing to teenagers by modernising it and making it more lively and busy. I chose a grey cat because I felt it wasn't as 'in your face' as, say, a ginger one would be. It also gives it a more relaxed and calmer atmosphere. I decided to reject this idea because I do not feel it would appeal to teenagers.

Snack Time!

Initial Ideas

There are various snacks that I can design to meet the needs of this project. The snacks that I produce must be suitable for swimmers and their diets. From my research, I know that the meals should contain mainly carbohydrate and protein. Hopefully, I will be able to adapt various dishes and snacks to contain higher amounts of carbohydrate and protein.

The dishes below can be eaten as snacks but some of them are main meals which I will adapt to snack portions.

Snack 1: Sandwich Selection

A selection of fresh sandwiches could be served every day at the sports centre. Unfortunately, most of the fillings wouldn't provide more than 5 g of carbohydrate. Various fillings would have to be served every day. 6/10

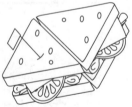

Snack 2: Jacket Potato and Filling

The filling that I think would be most suitable would either be tuna or chilli as these both contain protein. The potato also contains enough carbohydrate to meet the 5 g minimum requirement. However, if left to stand, the potatoes won't keep fresh and the filling may harden. 6/10

Snack 3: Smokey Bacon Spaghetti

This dish is a pasta dish which contains mainly bacon and tomatoes. The dish is colourful, appetising and easy to prepare. The cost of the snack is low as it is made from basic ingredients. I would give this dish 8/10 for meeting my specifications.

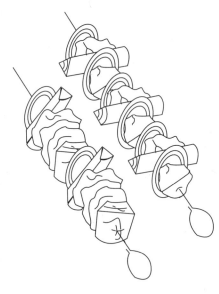

Snack 4: Mixed Grill Skewers

This snack is easy to cook and can be served with various side dishes. This dish doesn't contain more than 450 kcal. The portions of this dish can easily be adapted. People can ask for their required number of skewers. 7/10

Snack 5: Chinese Turkey Stir-Fry

This dish is full of colour and is very appetising. It could be served in snack portions or after exercise in main meal portions. The dish does exceed the cost limit. I don't think the dish would keep very well if left to stand. 5/10

Rag Doll

Design Ideas

lucy lou
A farmgirl

Checked shirt

Brown hat

Patch

Denim dungarees

Red coat

Plaits

Belt

Boots

Pinafore

Captain Matt
A pirate

Mary
A Victorian doll

Task 5 Action

Evaluation point

As you plan your initial ideas, this is an ideal opportunity for creating evidence of evaluation that you can write up into your final report.

How do your initial ideas meet the needs of your specification?

Which ideas would you choose for further development and why?

Summary of what you need to submit

A number of design sheets that contain a wide variety of initial ideas. At this stage, your proposals do not have to be too detailed.

Teacher review

Date submitted:

Teacher comments:

Targets for improvement:

Task 6

Developing your ideas
and adding more detail

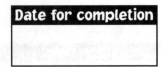

Developing some of your initial ideas

When you have produced your initial ideas, you need to work through them and decide which to develop and which to reject.

As your ideas emerge, some will stand out because they:

- best meet the requirements of your design specification

- are liked by your client

- look imaginative and different

- provide elegant solutions to problems.

Good design is about striking a balance between the optimal functional requirements of your product and the best visual appeal you can achieve. As you review your ideas, you will begin to see which designs offer the best opportunity for success.

Each idea may suggest something that can be used in your final design, so think about how you can pull together all of your good ideas.

Examples of development of design ideas are given on pages 68 to 75.

Modelling

As your design thinking develops, you will begin to realise that planning on paper has its limitations and you need to see how your ideas might look in a three-dimensional way or how new dishes you are planning might taste.

You may, for example, want to try modifying electronic circuits. Will they work? Will you need to change the values of components? Alternatively, your project may involve you changing ingredients in menus to produce different tastes or increased nutritional value.

This stage of your work is called **modelling** and it is concerned with working more directly with the materials you are hoping to use for your project. You may, instead, use an alternative technique or material which replicates your materials and processes in a cheaper and quicker way, eg using card, foam, or 'creating' onscreen in a software package. Designers use the term **mock-up** to describe this stage of the process.

You can model your ideas in order to try out different ways to resolve any problems and fine tune your designs when you have reached the limits of what you can achieve by drawing or writing. Some good examples of modelling include:

- Use of a software package to test out whether your circuit design will actually work.

- Use of card to create a model of a lever mechanism to test if it will work.

- Use of cheaper fabric to make up a prototype or toile to test if your pattern needs to be modified.

- Making a foam model to test out the size, form, ergonomics and anthropometrics of a new product, eg a mobile phone you might be designing.

Testing

As you get to the point where your designs and models take shape, it is essential to collect the views of your client before you proceed to the final development of your project.

You may also wish to ask others for their opinions, eg parents, friends, potential users, etc. You could set up a testing panel, for example, to discover which recipe or toy design is liked best. You should also test to see if your designs actually work, and that they are safe. The results could then be included in your design folder, along with photographs of the testing in progress or the designs you have tested.

An example of results from a testing panel is shown on pages 76 and 77.

Developing your designs towards a final proposal

Your final proposal needs to incorporate the best elements of your designs and should meet the requirements of your design specification to the best of your ability.

Now you need to plan in more detail and think about what you will need to know in order to make your product. At this stage, think about specific details and ask yourself precise questions, for example:

- What materials, ingredients or components are you going to use and why?

- What sizes, quantities and values of components will you need to use and why?

- What techniques will you use to make your final product and why have you selected these particular methods?

- Where will you obtain the materials to make your final product and how much is it likely to cost?

These questions could form the titles for sections within the design development part of your design folder. You may find that you need to undertake further research at this stage, particularly of making processes and materials.

An example of a final design is shown on page 78.

Industrial practices

Throughout your work, you need to provide evidence that you have considered how the design and making of your product would be affected if it were to be commercially produced. For example, what processes might be used in an industrial situation to manufacture the product you are designing? Would your product be produced as a 'one-off' item or is it capable of being batch or mass produced?

Look at the information on page 66 and see if you can identify which category your design product might fit. Check with your friends or your teacher if you need a second opinion.

Explain in your design folder which industrial method of production might be used to manufacture your design. What implications has this got for the cost of making and the likely costs to a potential customer? For example, consider whether it might be possible to mass produce your product by an automated production line, or whether it is better produced in smaller quantities by a hand-crafted approach. Whilst the set-up costs are higher for mass production, the running costs are often cheaper. Hand-made objects are expensive to produce, but are often cheaper to set up.

Industrial methods of production

One-off
Also known as **job production**

> This involves designing and making single products usually for a special order. This can also be known as a commission. For example, a fashion designer might produce a specially-ordered suit for an individual person. The process is usually labour-intensive and involves limited mechanisation. The products are usually very expensive.

Batch production
Also known as **small scale production** or **low volume production**

> This is where small quantities of the same product are made. They are usually made to order and there may be some opportunity for the client to select options that meet their needs. Some mechanisation and jigs may be used to improve accuracy and to speed up production. Examples of batch production include boat building, specialist sports cars, a range of bread produced by a local baker, and designer fashions.

Mass production
Also known as **repetitive flow** or **volume production**

> This involves producing large quantities of identical products. It may include mechanised or automated production lines. In many cases, special moulds, dyes and automated production lines may be used to speed up output. The production of large quantities of the same product reduces costs to the consumer. Televisions, computers, high street fashions, tins of baked beans, cola drinks and birthday cards are just a few examples of this enormous range.

You should also think about how each of the following might be relevant to your product in an industrial context, and how each might be undertaken:

- research and development which might include market research and the testing of prototypes
- meeting deadlines set by your clients
- different approaches to making which could include sub-contracting or the use of jigs/templates to aid marking out and promote accurate assembly
- independent testing which might include market trials
- the use of ICT to provide greater quality and accuracy in designing and making
- environmental issues – use of resources, waste disposal, pollution, recycling
- quality control and assurance
- health and safety issues including risk analysis.

INITIAL DESIGN

I have developed my initial design.
I wanted to make it a necklace pendant.
I decided to drop the very smallest
semi-circle as it would be fiddly to make.
I would join the circles with metal links.

Mahogany   Oak   Pine

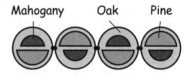

Stone   Nickel Silver   Brass

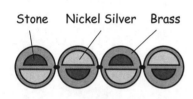

Beech   Oak   Pine

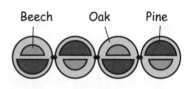

Stone   Nickel Silver   Brass

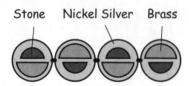

Stone   Nickel Silver   Brass

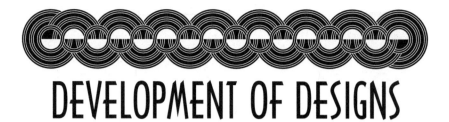

DEVELOPMENT OF DESIGNS

FINAL DESIGN

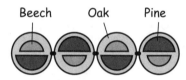

Beech   Oak   Pine

This is my final design. I have chosen to do it in wood as I think it will be different, so more attractive. I also prefer working with wood. I will be using three different types of wood. This design was actually influenced by the border on this page, which is from the later Art Deco period. By using wood, the design will be comfortable, cheap and lightweight.

» I really like the idea of using wood. It is different and the natural finish will look attractive. I also think it will be more comfortable to wear. I think the design is very balanced as well. It looks good! «

CLIENT'S VIEW

69

Development of Designs

Initial design

This is a simple figure. I will adapt his feet to be round wooden cylinders, so he can roll or be pushed along the ground. As he rolls, I would like his hat to go up and down.

The hat

This is the original hat. I thought it could be made more appealing for a young child.

This is my final design. I added a flower, to be painted in simple primary colours, as I thought it gave more fun to the toy.

I decided to give it more shape, but thought that as it was a moving part it still needed more appeal.

Mechanical Toy

A handle

I decided to add a handle to the toy, in order to make the toy easier to push along for a child and also to add stability. I rejected the first design because it would be difficult to make safe and it would be tricky for young children to grasp. Similarly the second, although safe, might not be good for younger people. The final design I think should be easy to grasp by the youngest of children.

The mechanism

This is the cam that I initially thought of. It will produce a gradual rise and then a sudden drop. However, after some consideration, I decided that a gradual rise and a gradual drop would be more suitable. My research tells me that this cam would produce such an effect.

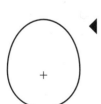

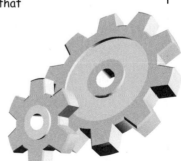

style café

design development

For wheelchair access, I have brought the door to the front. I have also added a wall – the front is not just a glass window. I think the idea is very possible and also practical. The idea for this large window originally comes from a café in Cambridge which I photographed in my research. It is only a small café but the full glass front makes it appear a lot bigger. This is my aim for the café. I think this theme is very original and also fascinating. I have kept the colours nearly the same and my client loves it. She explains that she loves to be able to see inside and out of the café.

I placed the café's products on the window to add colour and information, and to attract customers. However, my client dislikes this, so I will place this information on a billboard outside.

style café

final design

I wanted to keep the window figure from my original design because my client and I liked it so much. It also keeps the window interesting and unusual. My client suggested that I etch the figure onto the glass instead of using paint so as not to block the customers' view.

I decided to leave out the name 'Style Café', because I wanted my café and nightclub to have the same name, so I just used 'The Balcony'.

I used Microsoft® Word to design some initial ideas for the name 'The Balcony' but in the end I preferred to use my own style of painting, which also achieves uniqueness.

Development of Ted
the Tortoise

I tried out some different grins for my tortoise. I like the final one as it makes him look warm, funny and a bit cheeky for the reader.

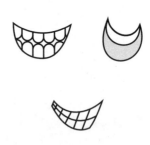

I didn't like these legs and shoes so I changed them to make them neater and also more interesting. The new legs look more in proportion, and the rounded shoes are softer and friendlier.

I wasn't very keen on the gloves I had drawn. I drew these mittens, which I think look better. They make the character seem softer and nicer.

I tried out another face but this looks a bit angry because of the eyebrows, and is not very interesting.

Ted the Tortoise seems like a good character. The colours go well I think, especially the contrast between the dark green and the lighter colours of the shell. The face seems friendly and inviting for a young child. The round eyes and eyebrows make him look happy and the grin lights up the picture. I think watercolours would definitely look best. They have a sketchy look which is quite effective.

Snack Time!

Smokey Bacon Spaghetti

One of the reasons why I chose this pasta dish is because it was one of the highest voted for in the questionnaire. I initially thought of this dish because it is both colourful and appetising but cheap and easy to prepare. Once I had made the dish I realised how easy it is to prepare and make. To test how good my re-designed snack was I decided to set up a tasting panel.

Name

E Barnard

R Castle

T Clarke

L Edwards

A Fleet

P Middleton

F Stanbridge

J Smith

G Thomas

M Woodcraft

Comments

As you can see from the table below, the snack was very successful with all of the tasters. One reason I think my snack was so successful was because of the adaptations I made to the recipe — adding mushrooms and pepper to give extra taste and texture.

I think I planned my meal sufficiently, enabling all of my ingredients to be cooked for the right amount of time. This ensured that the meal was presented in the best possible way.

I feel that the sauce was slightly greasy, due to the extra oil produced from frying the bacon. Although nobody commented on this, I would reduce the fat content in future by not adding the extra sunflower oil.

Taste	Appearance	Texture	Overall
10	9	9	9
9	8	8	8
8	9	9	9
10	9	10	10
10	8	9	9
9	10	10	10
8	7	9	8
9	8	9	9
10	9	8	9
7	8	8	8

Rag Doll

Final Design

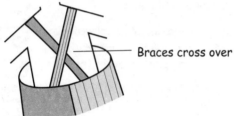

Braces cross over

View from back

Yellow hair

Red gloves

Hoop in trousers

Stripey blue

Plain red

Clarence the Clown

Task 6 Action

Evaluation point

As your ideas emerge and you make changes and modifications, this is an ideal opportunity for further evidence of evaluation that you can write up into your final report.

Give your reasons for choosing/rejecting your ideas.

What changes have you made during design development?
How will these changes improve your product?

Show how you have resolved any conflicting design demands.

What are the opinions of your client?

Summary of what you need to submit

1   A variety of design sheets where you have refined your initial ideas in more detail.

2   Examples of different types of modelling which help you and your client decide which designs may be the most suitable.

3   Evaluation comments from you and your client, explaining why you have developed some ideas in preference to others.

4   Your final design proposal.

Teacher review

Date submitted:

Teacher comments:

Targets for improvement:

Task 7

Planning and preparing
for making

Preparing to make your product

Once you have completed your designing and developed your
ideas into a final proposal, there are a few final details you need to
complete before you start to make your product:

- Produce a final plan of what you intend to make. Create
detailed plan drawings of your product, and if necessary a
scale model. You should provide enough detail for another
person to be able to make your product unaided. Include
dimensions, different views, details of materials to be used,
how the parts fit together, etc.

- Produce a list of all of the materials, ingredients or
components you will require to make your project –
including costings.

- Obtain the materials you will use for the product, either
from school or by purchasing them from a specialist shop.

- Consider what equipment you will need to make your
product. Is this available in your school?

- Identify any new skills or processes you will need to use
during your making. More importantly, consider whether
your teacher might be able to introduce you to any new
techniques. Has your school got the resources to make
your product?

- Note any constraints, eg availability of equipment or
materials, and work out how this can be overcome.

- Plan how you will use your time for making to ensure you
can work within your timescale.

Your final plan

Your final plan will take different forms depending upon the material area in which you are working, for example:

Electronic Products	Circuit diagram of the electronic part of the project and a working drawing of the container you intend to make to store the circuit.
Food Technology	Recipe and instructions (see pages 84 and 85 for an example).
Graphic Products	A model, perhaps to scale, or a drawing, template or net of your final idea.
Resistant Materials Technology	A working drawing of your product (see page 90 for an example).
Textiles Technology	A pattern of your garment (see pages 86 and 87 for an example).
Systems and Control Technology	A circuit diagram (electronic and/or pneumatic), and a working drawing.

Planning for making

In order to produce a plan of your time for making, you have to try to predict the processes you will be using to make your product and the time it will take to complete the different stages.

You may find this easier if you draw up a table with the headings shown on pages 82 and 83. You can either draw these out onto several sheets of A3 paper or you could design a table on your computer and update the information as your work progresses.

Planning for making table

Process	Tools/equipment	Estimated time
In this column, describe the stages in making your product. For example, begin by talking about how you might mark out your work or weigh your ingredients.	In this column, list all the specialist equipment you need to have to complete your work relating to each process.	Estimate how long it will take to complete this stage of the making.

For example:

Marking out	*Pencil, lightbox, fine permanent marker, cartridge paper and dressmaking pins*	*1$^1/_4$ hours*

Actual time	Explanation	Comments
How long did this process actually take compared with your estimate?	In this column, explain, using notes and sketches, how you will complete the process.	Use this column to record how your work progressed and to what extent the process was completed to a good standard. If things go wrong, explain how you overcame the difficulties. Use the comments in this column to help write your evaluation report.

1³⁄₄ hours	*I will trace my design from the pattern onto cartridge paper using the lightbox. I will pin this onto my fabric before cutting out my shape.*	*This stage went as expected except that the small pins I used were difficult to stick through the cartridge paper and the heavy fabric. I decided to use some pins which were longer and stronger. This was more successful.*

An example of such a table is shown on pages 88 and 89.

Snack Time!

Planning for Making Smokey Bacon Spaghetti

Ingredients (to serve 4)

30 ml sunflower oil
2 cloves of crushed garlic
175 g smoked, rindless streaky bacon, chopped
2 x 400 g cans of chopped tomatoes
230 g spaghetti
1 tbsp tomato purée
3 tbsp fresh mixed herbs, chopped
freshly grated parmesan to taste

Equipment List

- Chopping board
- Garlic crusher
- Sharp knife
- Two large pans
- Tablespoon
- Stirring spoon
- Sieve

Costing

30 ml sunflower oil	£0.04
2 cloves of garlic	£0.01
175 g smoked, rindless bacon	£0.96
2 x 400 g cans of tomatoes	£0.34
230 g spaghetti	£0.22
1 tbsp tomato purée	£0.02
3 tbsp fresh mixed herbs	£0.04
freshly grated parmesan	£0.05
Total	**£1.68**

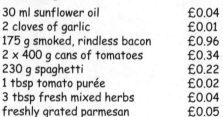

Step by Step Plan

1
Heat the oil in a saucepan.
Add the garlic and bacon.
Fry for 5 minutes.

2
Stir in the tomatoes, tomato purée, herbs and
seasoning. Bring to the boil, then cover and simmer
gently for 15 minutes, until the sauce has thickened.

3
Meanwhile, cook the spaghetti in a large saucepan
of boiling water for 8-10 minutes.

4
Drain the spaghetti, transfer to a plate and pour
the sauce over. Sprinkle parmesan cheese on top.

The Rag Doll

Plan for Making
Clown trousers

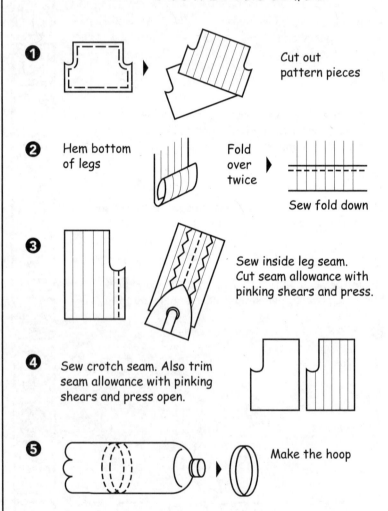

1 Cut out pattern pieces

2 Hem bottom of legs   Fold over twice ▸ Sew fold down

3 Sew inside leg seam. Cut seam allowance with pinking shears and press.

4 Sew crotch seam. Also trim seam allowance with pinking shears and press open.

5 Make the hoop

Hoop inside

6 Cut the top of the trousers with pinking shears. Then fold over and sew with hoop in place.

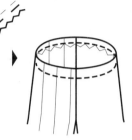

7 Attach braces. Secure at crossover point on back.

8 Cut front ends of braces diagonally. Attach buttons at the same time as the braces.

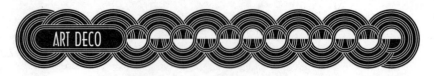

PLANNING FOR MAKING

BROOCH

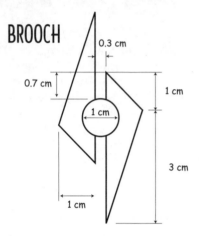

PROCESS	TOOLS/EQUIPMENT	TIME
Filing	File Emery paper	30 mins Week 4
Shaping the metal	Metal rod Hammer	15 mins Week 4
Soldering	Sulphuric acid Soldering torch Silver solder wire Flux File	30 mins Week 5

EARRINGS

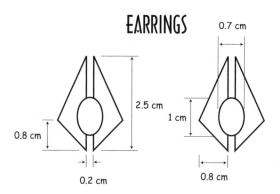

0.7 cm

2.5 cm

1 cm

0.8 cm

0.2 cm

0.8 cm

EXPLANATION

I needed to file the piece of metal that was to be the bezel around the stone.

I now had to shape the bezel into a ring shape. To do this, I hammered the piece of metal gently around the rod to form a ring.

I first had to put all the bits of metal into a bath of sulphuric acid before I soldered them. Then I placed a piece of solder either side of the gap in the ring and blasted it with heat until the solder melted. (Before soldering I coated the ring in flux.) I soldered the ring onto the base with the same process. (Before soldering the ring to the base, I filed away the surplus solder.)

COMMENTS

This went relatively well and I finished on time.

I was a bit nervous about this but once I started I found it quite easy to do.

My teacher helped me to begin with as I was a little apprehensive. It was quite fiddly but not difficult and I didn't really have any problems.

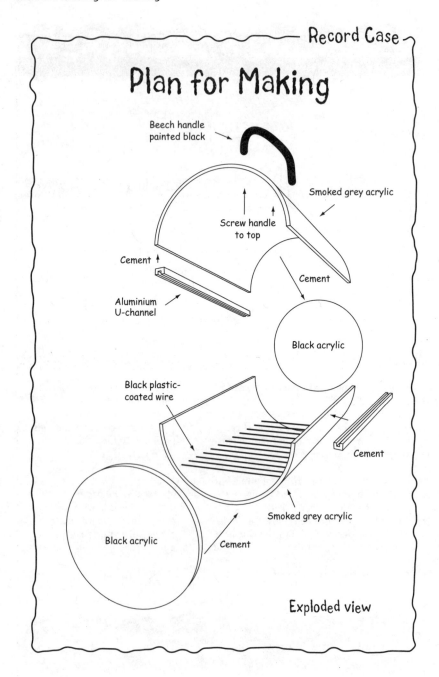

Record Case

Plan for Making

Beech handle painted black

Smoked grey acrylic

Screw handle to top

Cement

Cement

Aluminium U-channel

Black acrylic

Black plastic-coated wire

Cement

Black acrylic

Cement

Smoked grey acrylic

Exploded view

Task 7 Action

Evaluation point

As your planning develops, what have you decided to change and why? How have these changes improved your product? Have you had any problems?

Explain how your product could be mass produced.

Summary of what you need to submit

1   A plan for making.

2   A list of the materials, ingredients, equipment and components you need to make your final product including sizes, quantities and costings.

3   Detailed scale drawings, models, circuit diagrams, patterns, templates or jigs to assist in the making of your final project.

Teacher review

Date submitted:

Teacher comments:

Targets for improvement:

Task 8

Making your chosen product

Modifying your plan

Your planning for making will usually need to be changed or modified in some way as your making progresses. This is inevitable and you should not think that modification of your plan will either lose you marks or be seen as getting it wrong. When you begin projects such as this, you will find that you have to change your approach as the work progresses because:

- you under-estimate or over-estimate the time it will take you

- you find different ways of making the product that you did not know about during your designing

- processes you try out do not work as well as you had hoped; consequently, you have to modify these to make your product more successful

- during your making, you use different materials to those you had originally planned, as they seem to be better suited to the product.

You can make as many changes as you want during the making process, provided that these changes result in a better final product. This is a natural part of the ongoing evaluation of your work. As long as you can justify these changes in your evaluation, you should see this as a very positive part of your designing.

Remember that manufacturing is not just about making things, it is about making things:

- simpler
- more cheaply
- more environmentally friendly.

- more quickly
- more efficiently

Developing quality into your making

When we buy products as consumers, we would always expect them to be of a certain quality. The term 'quality' can be a difficult one to understand so you need to consider how it influences products to be able to then apply this within your own making.

Listed below you will find some of the features you would expect from a quality product. However, different products will have different qualities. If you were developing a food product then taste would be an important quality you would be testing. However, if you were making a storage unit, then taste would not be an issue!

Aspects of quality

Ask yourself these questions about your product as your making progresses:

- Is your product being made accurately? Are your measurements/quantities/cooking times being carefully checked and amended if incorrect?

- Are the processes you use to make your product being carefully monitored and evaluated to make sure you get the results you expect? If you are not getting the results you expect, how are you trying to improve the situation?

- Collect other people's opinions of your product as it develops – especially your client's. Modify your work accordingly.

- Check your emerging product against your design specification. Does it still meet your original intentions or is it, perhaps, better?

Keeping a record of change

Keep a record of any changes you make to your work as this will contribute towards your evaluation report. Explain why you make any changes and how this has improved your product.

Industrial processes

Projects you make at school are not directly comparable with products made in an industrial setting. This is usually because most industrial set-ups are geared to making items in quantity rather than one-off prototypes similar to your project. However, this should not stop you from considering how your product could be made on an industrial scale, as well as the ways in which jigs and templates could assist in the making of quality products for a large market. You should continue to consider industrial methods of production and how the techniques used in industry could meet your requirements.

Task 8 Action

Evaluation point

As your product emerges and you review its quality, this is an ideal opportunity for further evidence of evaluation that you can write up into your final report.

What changes have you made during making? How have these changes improved your product?

Summary of what you need to submit

Your completed product made to the highest possible standard, supported with any jigs, templates or simple prototypes which you have developed to help your design thinking and decision making.

Teacher review

Date submitted:

Teacher comments:

Targets for improvement:

Task 9

Testing and evaluating
your work

Writing your evaluation report

Your evaluation report is a collection of the thoughts, reflections
and judgements you have made during both the designing and
making stages of your project. In particular, consider how these
choices and changes to your work have improved the final
outcome and what you have learnt from this experience which will
make you a better designer in the future.

Examples of evaluation reports are provided on pages 100 to 105.

You might consider splitting your report into two sections to reflect
the two different stages of the process, ie:

1   **Evaluating throughout the process of designing and
    making.** This includes evaluating the appropriateness of
    your starting point, your initial research, design ideas,
    development, plan of making and the actual making of
    your product.

2   **Testing and evaluating the performance of your final
    product.** For this to be thorough, your project needs to be
    completed and capable of being tested and evaluated by
    the client, in the environment for which it was designed.

The process of designing and making

This is not a description or diary of what you did, or how you did it. This part of your report should focus upon those aspects of your designing and making where you had to make choices about your project or reconsider your proposed intentions. If you pull together the comments you have made in response to the evaluation points of this handbook, you will find that you can write a couple of sentences or a paragraph on each of the parts of your project. Use sketches or photographs to support your views and opinions.

Consider the following questions:

Designing

- Explain your reasons for selecting your starting point. If you were to tackle this project again, would you still think it was a suitable choice? If not, what would you do next time around?

- Discuss the most successful and least successful parts of your research. Were there any significant gaps in your research that you discovered as the project developed?

- Was your design specification as detailed as it should have been? What might you have added?

- Did your initial ideas meet your design specification?

- Which ideas did you choose to develop and why?

- What were the views of your client about your initial and developed ideas?

- What were the most important/successful features of your final design?

- What were the least successful features?

- Did your final design fully meet your design specification?

- Did you leave anything out of your design specification?

Making

- Why did you choose the particular materials, ingredients or components for your final product?

- Would you reconsider the materials and processes you used due to problems you encountered whilst making?

- During the making of the project, what parts were you pleased with and why?

- What aspects of your making could be improved and how?

- What new skills did you learn? Did your lack of experience in the application of these skills limit the quality of your work?

- How did you manage the time available for this project? Could you manage your time more efficiently in future projects?

- If you were to repeat the designing and making of this project, what would you do differently second time around?

Evaluating and testing the final product

Here are a set of questions you might ask about your work when you are evaluating and testing the final product. Write a sentence or paragraph about each of these questions to produce your final report. Use sketches or photographs to support your statements.

Consider the following questions:

- Look critically at your final product. What do you believe to be its strengths and weaknesses?

- Does it work as you had intended? If not, why not? To what extent does it meet your proposed intention?

- Is it easy to use?

- Have problems arisen due to constraints around materials or your limited skills and expertise?

- Does the visual appeal of the product match the intended vision of your final design? If not, why not?

- Test out your product in the most appropriate way. Gather the opinions of your client(s).

- Does your product meet the needs of your client(s)?

- Is your product cost-effective?

- Are there any environmental concerns?

- How could your product be improved? You could include sketches of your proposed improvements.

Final note about your evaluation report

When writing evaluation reports, remember that you are reflecting upon what you have learnt about designing and making as a result of the project. Your teacher or the examiner does not want to hear "… everything went well!" – as we all know, this is not what happens in the real world.

Your teacher and the examiners are looking for your ability to analyse the project. You need to draw out, in a thoughtful and critical way, those aspects of your work which informed your thinking and prompted changes in direction. It is this flexibility and confidence to make sensible changes in direction as your work evolves which will signal that you are a good designer and also impress the people who mark your work.

Rag Doll

Evaluation

I am really proud of my doll (Clarence the Clown). I think he is very appealing. I also really enjoyed making him.

The doll itself was not too difficult to do, except sewing the soles of the feet and the hair. This eventually worked though.

I am pleased with the doll's face as it is bright and bold – just as I wanted it to be. I am also especially pleased with the way the hair eventually turned out.

Making the trousers was moderately easy. I learnt a lot of new skills making these, such as how to join the crotch seam together.

To improve the trousers, I could have overlocked the raw edges rather than just cutting them with pinking shears. I feel the overlocking looks better but I am not sure about the relative effectiveness.

I also think that I could have used either a striped fabric that kept its shape more or a red fabric which 'gave' more. This might have made it easier to work with the two fabrics. The problem with the two I used was that the area of the hoop the red fabric took up was larger as it gathered less easily. This makes it look slightly lopsided. I tried to put creases into the red fabric to make it stay and this improved it a little.

When I made the shoes, I didn't thoroughly think through the method of fastening/removing the shoes. I knew I wanted laces; the problem was that the method I was going to use was not suitable for the shoes as they get narrower at the top. I had to adapt the way I put the laces in. It worked out in the end though. If I made the shoes again, I would use a different pattern.

The piece of clothing I found hardest was the shirt, particularly the arms, which eventually turned out slightly longer than I had imagined. There are a few pleats in the arms but they are not noticeable as they are fairly gathered anyway.

When making the back, the velcro was really difficult to get right. It was also hard to sew on and get straight.

I learnt how to sew on bias binding around the neck hole. This took me quite a long time, particularly the slip stitch which is even, although it is a little large.

The neck hole was originally going to be curved but I cut it wrong and it ended up as a 'V' neck. Luckily, when I used the bias binding it went curved again.

ART DECO

EVALUATION

CLIENT'S VIEW

❝ I thought that the jewellery looked very attractive, was very well made and had some pleasing shapes and colours. The earrings were perhaps a little too heavy to be used for long-term wear but would be good just for evening wear. I thought that all the jewellery reflected the Art Deco period very well and corresponded with designs I had seen in books. The brooch was lovely and was very versatile as it could be worn in different positions to give quite different effects. All pieces of jewellery had been carefully made with a meticulous attention to detail. I thought the materials used were appropriate and the finished product would be durable and hard-wearing. I would be prepared to pay up to £10 for the set of earrings and brooch. I think that there is a very great need for this as there seems to be a large gap in the market where Art Deco jewellery is concerned. ❞

MY COMMENTS

I think that my product is cost-effective. The materials I have used are all relatively cheap and easily obtained, although the stones are harder to find than the pieces of metal as you need to go to a specialist shop. I could change the materials used to more expensive materials but my target market would prefer a cheaper, more reasonably priced product. The jewellery is environmentally friendly – it doesn't give off any harmful gases whilst being made, and the materials used are obtained without any major effects on the environment. I have used glue which is very hard-wearing so the product will be sturdy and safe. Where possible, I have soldered as this is stronger than glue.

I think that my project fulfilled the design brief. My client thought that making Art Deco jewellery was a really good idea as it filled a gap in the market and also because the Art Deco style is coming back into fashion. I think that my jewellery is eye-catching and attractive. The colours of the metal and stones work well together and complement each other. The different shapes are proportional to each other so don't look odd. This type of jewellery would be suitable for sale in a craft fair or specialist hand-made jewellery shop.

Evaluation

I am very satisfied with the toy I have completed. I have tried out my toy at school and at home with people of different ages. The toy performs well as it moves along a flat surface. I was very pleased as the mechanism in the toy also works as well over a bumpy surface. I made quite a few modifications to the toy, from the initial idea to the final idea:

1   I decided to add a flower to the hat.

2   I decided to change the shape of the cam. This change made the hat rise more steadily and efficiently.

3   I changed the length and shape of the handle. Safety aspects and the height of a young child influenced this decision.

I think all of these modifications have improved my final design. I researched into many areas concerning toys and what's on the market. I looked at various mechanisms and I think I chose the best one to suit my design.

The toy was made out of a mixture of materials. The main material was 9 mm birch-faced plywood. To mark out the holes for drilling, I stuck the two faces of the toy together with double-sided sticky tape to make it more accurate. However, as I tried to take them apart, the tape was so strong that some of the birch veneer split. It took a lot of preparing and sanding to disguise these damages.

Mechanical Toy

One of the final stages of making the toy was the painting of it. Before I painted the toy, I tested out different colours on a scrap piece of wood, to see what colour they dried. I decided not to paint the wheels because, after a lot of wear and tear, the paint would soon chip. Instead, I varnished them.

Whilst designing and making the toy, I had to think about safety aspects for children. Unfortunately, the axle was made out of welding rod. About 5 mm of welding rod sticks out on each side of the wheels. This sharp edge would inevitably be a safety hazard for young children. If I were to make the toy again, I would cover each side with a smooth, plastic cap.

Overall, I think the project has been very successful. Although the toy is large, it is quite light and it could be easily marketed. In my experience, children don't have high tolerance levels and don't always play with toys carefully. I think my toy is very sturdy, and it would take a large force or an adult hand to damage it.

I feel that my design has met the requirements of the design brief. The toy is attractive to the eye. I think a child of age three to five years would enjoy playing with it. I used some of the best materials available to me and the toy clearly contains a mechanism (a cam).

Task 9 Action

Evaluation point

Draw together all the evaluation you have made throughout your project, and collect the opinions of your client.

Summary of what you need to submit

An evaluation report which looks critically at your designing and making and which examines the strengths, weaknesses and suitability of your final product.

Teacher review

Date submitted:

Teacher comments:

Targets for improvement:

Useful Web sites

BBC	http://www.bbc.co.uk/
British Nutrition Foundation	http://www.nutrition.org.uk/
British Standards Institution BSI – Safety Guides	http://www.bsi.org.uk/
Cadbury	http://www.cadbury.co.uk/
Design and Technology Association	http://www.data.org.uk/
Design Council	http://www.design-council.org.uk/
Electronic Circuit Design	http://www.crocodile-clips.com/
Farnell Electronics	http://www.farnell.com/
Food Allergy Network	http://www.foodallergy.org/
Fresh Fruit and Vegetable Information Bureau	http://www.ffvib.co.uk/
IKEA Stores	http://www.ikea.com/
Lego	http://www.lego.com/
Levi's Clothing	http://www.levi.com/
Maplin Electronics	http://www.maplin.co.uk/
Ministry of Agriculture	http://www.maff.gov.uk/
PCB Design Package	http://www.new-wave-concepts.com/
The Fresh Food Company	http://www.freshfood.co.uk/
Trading Standards	http://www.tradingstandards.gov.uk/
UN Food and Agriculture Organisation	http://www.fao.org/
Vegetarian Pages	http://www.veg.org/veg/
Zanussi	http://www.zanussi.com/

Glossary

Aesthetics An appreciation of whether an object is pleasing or not. How our senses react to the object. This can often be dominated by our visual responses – how good it looks. However, other senses such as hearing, smell, touch and perhaps taste will contribute to our overall aesthetic reaction and response.

Analyse This is concerned with looking in detail at reference material or products to help you discover more information about them. How do they work? What ingredients do they contain? What are their essential features? How might they be made?

Analysis This will be the results of your observations. It may be a written account of your findings. It may also take the form of a series of sketches through which you have been analysing the shape and form of a particular product.

Annotated sketches These are design drawings that include explanatory notes to help the designer communicate more effectively with the client. They provide additional written information to support the drawings, for example, the type of material from which the product can be made, the name and colour of parts, or constructional details.

Anthropometric data This provides detailed information related to the dimensions of the human body. Designers can use this information at the developmental stage of their designing. This helps to determine accurate measurements for their products to ensure they will be comfortable and capable of adjustment to suit the needs of a variety of users.

Artefact A product which has been made by people rather than a product of nature.

Batch production This is where the manufacturer produces small quantities of similar products, eg local baker, small boat-builder, specialist car manufacturer. Mechanisation may be used in the process. For example, jigs and moulds may be used to speed up the process and make the products more precisely and more efficiently.

CAD (computer aided design) The production of detailed drawings prior to making is one of the most time-consuming parts of the process. Each time a part is modified, new drawings have to be produced. Changes can easily be made on a CAD system and the drawing can be sent to a CAM output for making.

CAM (computer aided manufacture) A variety of machines such as a lathe, milling machine, sewing machine, embroiderer and plotter can download and make items designed on a CAD system. CAM products are very precise, easy to produce and can be manufactured within a semi-automated environment.

Components list A list of items or parts which are required to make a product. It will include specific details including descriptions of components, sizes, materials and quantities.

Consumer The intended user of a particular product. We are all consumers. However, we have different factors which influence our choice. These include cost and the different requirements we might have for the performance of the product.

Consumer Association This is an independent organisation that produces reports on products and services. The Consumer Association magazine *Which?* is published once a month and contains the results and analysis of a range of products including their recommended 'Best Buys'. *Which?* is available on subscription and you can find copies in most libraries.

Consumer survey A way of finding out the views of potential customers or people who have already used a product. You may use a questionnaire and then analyse the responses.

Design brief A concise statement which sets out the task, ie the problem to be solved.

Design criteria A set of performance characteristics against which a product might be judged.

Design proposal A variety of suggested solutions indicating how the design brief might be resolved.

Design specification A detailed list of precise requirements which the product must achieve if it is to be successful.

Ergonomics A study of the way people interact with designed products, systems or environments. Ergonomic information is used to ensure that products are safe, comfortable and easy to use.

Flow chart A method of listing your procedures for completing a specific task. The different procedures can be placed into boxes which are then put in order to demonstrate the flow through the process.

Form An object which is three-dimensional as opposed to a shape which is two-dimensional. For example, a cube is a form; a square is a shape.

Market segment This is the name given to the identified group of people who may purchase certain products. Economic use of advertising will target campaigns in the newspapers and magazines that this group read and in the commercial breaks of the TV programmes they are likely to watch.

Market tests/trials This is an aspect of market research whereby a small number of potential consumers are asked to evaluate new products prior to their launch on the market.

Marketing This is the process of promoting goods through advertising and packaging. People who work in marketing create an image for the product which ties in with the needs and aspirations of a particular group of consumers they intend to target, eg teenage girls, football supporters, old age pensioners, etc.

Mass production This involves manufacturing large quantities of the same product. The product can be part of a production line process whereby it moves through a number of stages in manufacture. At one time, many people were employed on production lines. However, many companies now use automation in some way to increase production and reduce costs.

Modelling This is the way in which we try to resolve our ideas as they emerge. Drawing is a form of two-dimensional modelling. Three-dimensional models can be made in card or foam. Recipes can be tried out on a small scale; different ingredients might be added to model their effects on the final dish. Fashion garments may be modelled to scale or made up in a cheaper fabric to resolve technical issues such as size and cut.

One-off This involves designing and making single products usually for a special order or to meet a specific need. These products tend to be expensive due to the high expenditure of time and the relatively low levels of mechanisation. The designer and maker may often be the same person.

Organoleptic quality A stimulus which affects the senses. This is particularly true of food when we experience the aroma, taste and texture of a product and we are able to describe and evaluate our feelings.

Primary source When collecting information, this relates to the original source of the information. For example, a questionnaire you have designed and then analysed is a primary source – you were the first person to create the data. This is compared with questionnaire data you may have collected from a book or other point of reference which was produced by someone else. This is then a **secondary source** of information.

Prototype This is a product that has been modelled to meet the requirements of your design problem. As part of the development stage of the process, it is made to test whether your product will be successful or whether it needs further modification.

Quality The overall impression of the quality of a product can be determined by a variety of factors including the technical performance and reliability of the product, the precision of manufacture, sympathetic use of materials and the overall aesthetics of the product.

Quality assurance This relates to monitoring and testing at different stages during production to ensure the required manufacturing standards are being maintained.

Questionnaire A survey which is used to find out people's responses to specific questions you need to answer to help guide your thinking.

Sensory descriptions This is a collection of adjectives which you can use to describe the way your senses react to certain situations. For example, when tasting and testing food, you can describe appearance, aroma, flavour, texture and after-taste as bitter, sweet, crunchy, smooth, acidic, granular, flaky, etc.

Style The way in which a product relates, through the way it looks, to particular times in history, for example, Art Deco. New styles can be made by combining those of previous periods and taking the best of each to provide a new look for a given product.

Taste test This is where you provide a group of people with the opportunity to taste a food or dish in order to collect their views and reactions about their likes and dislikes of the sample.